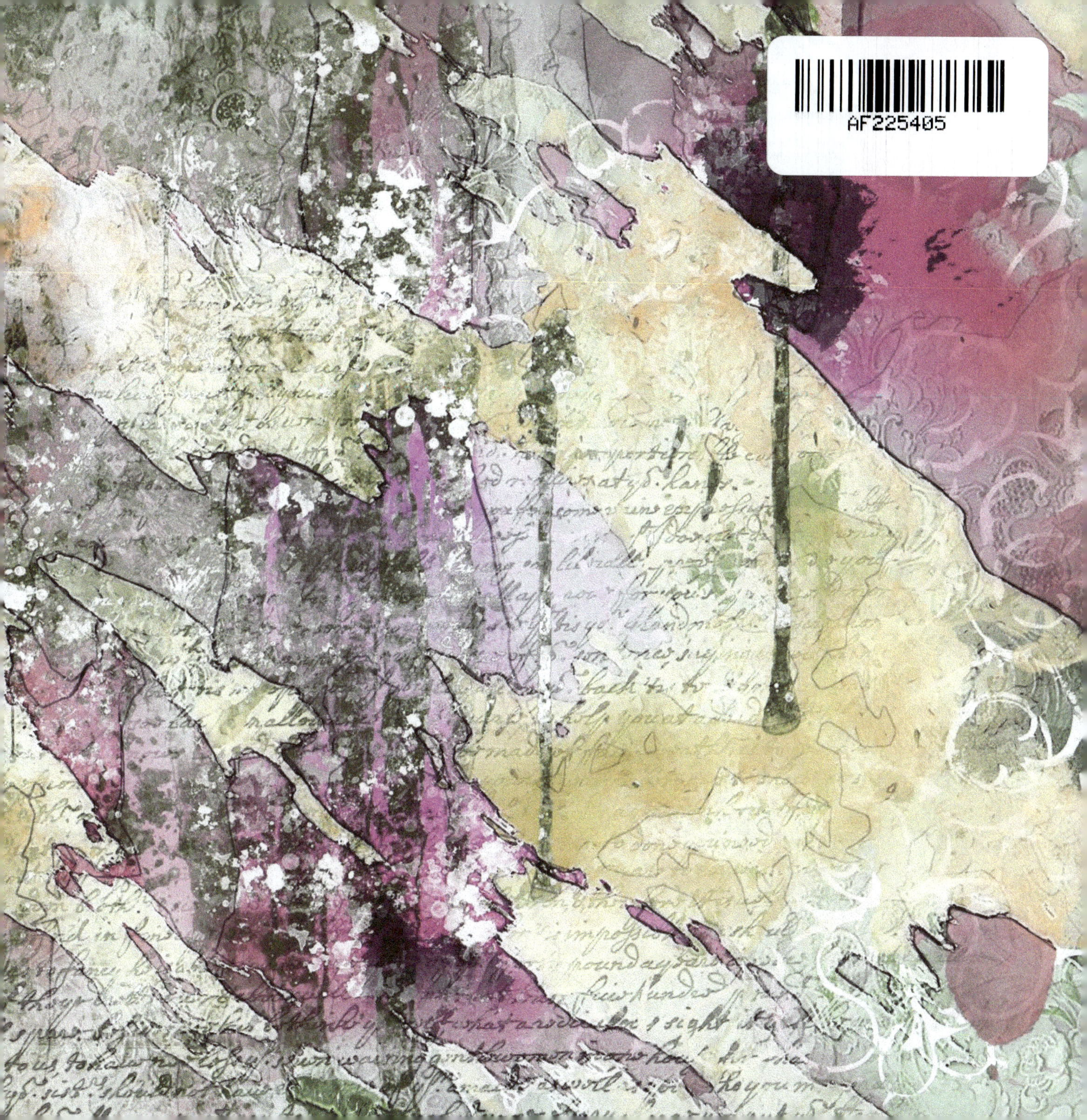

AF225405

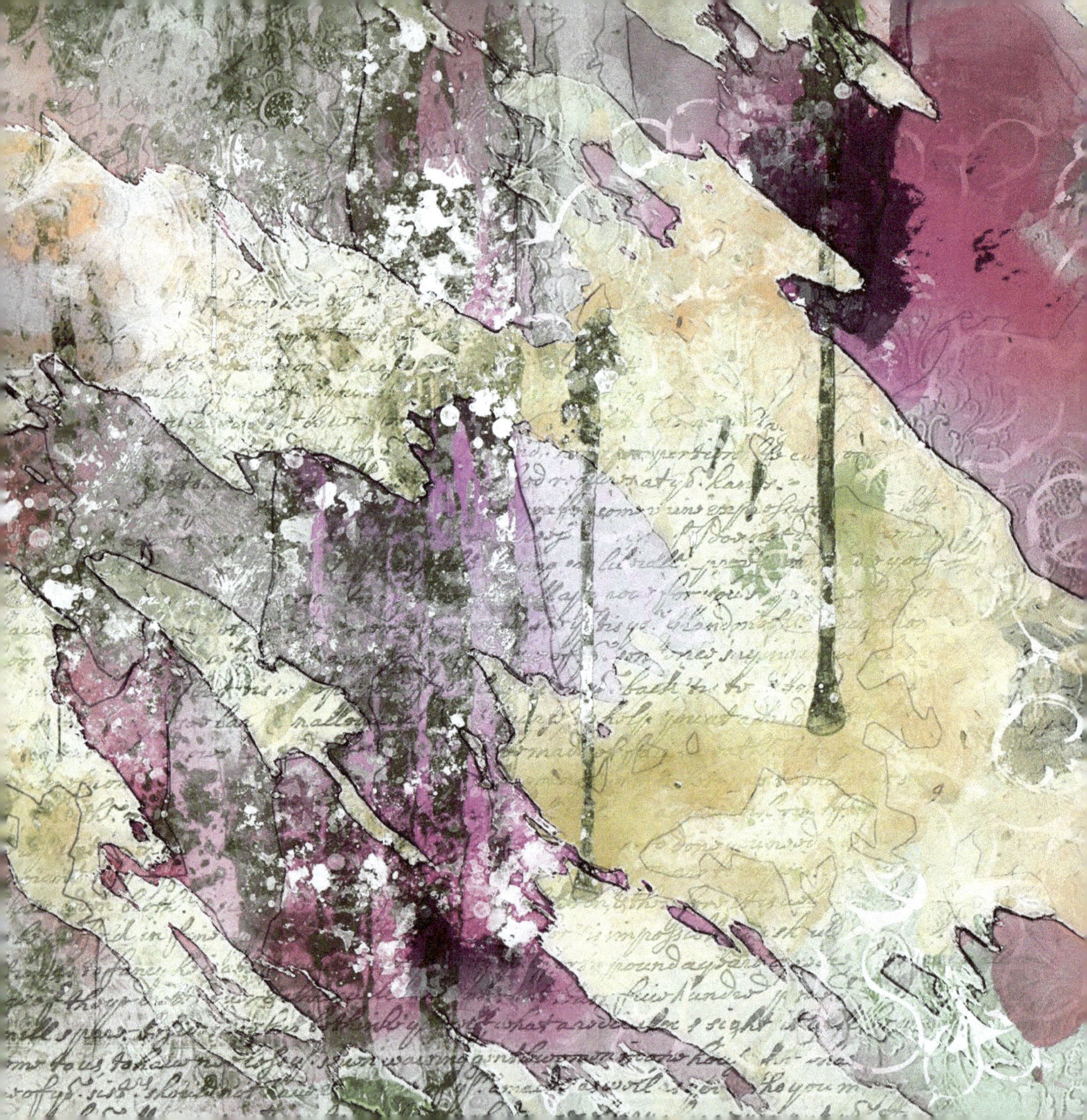

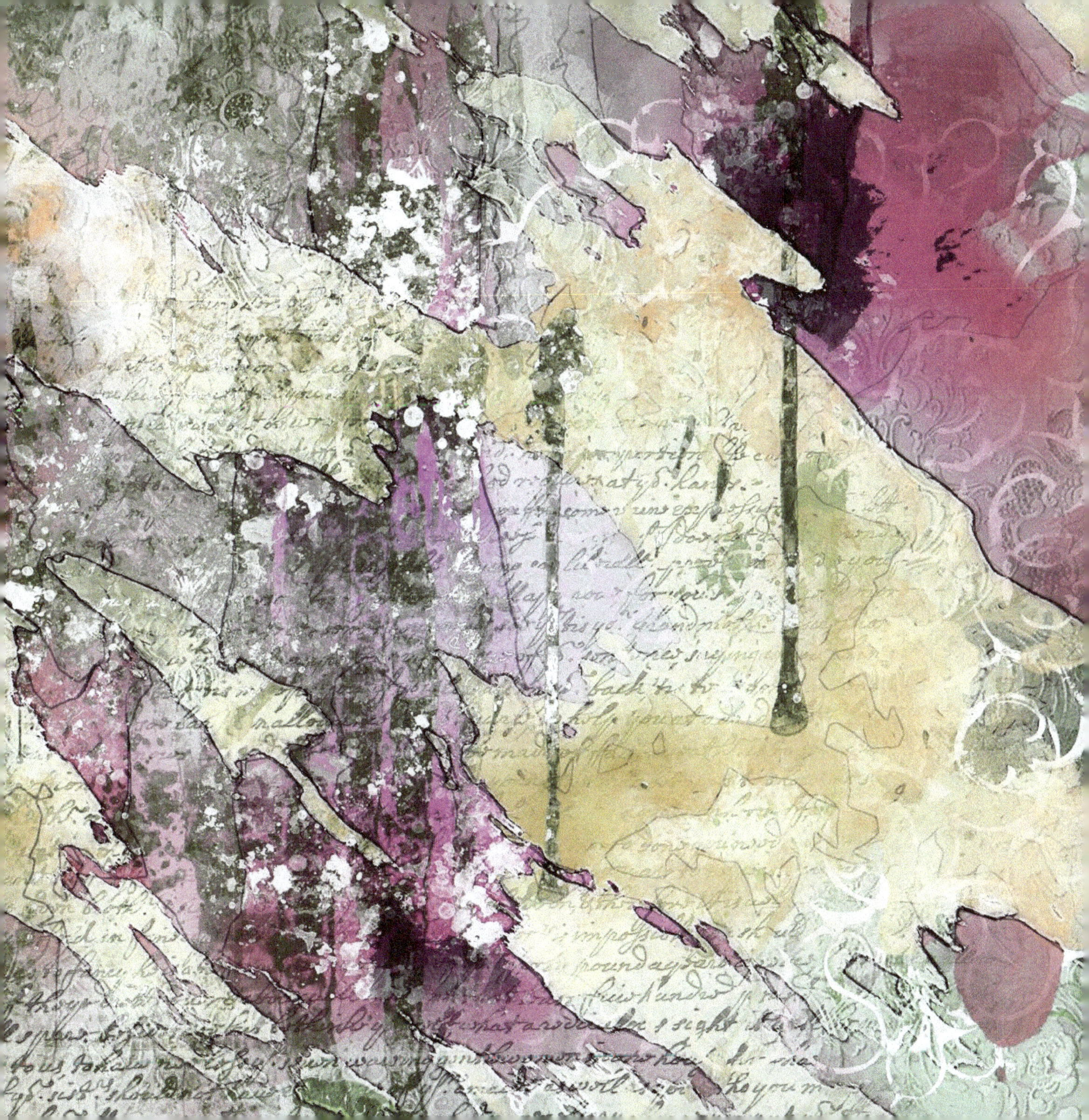

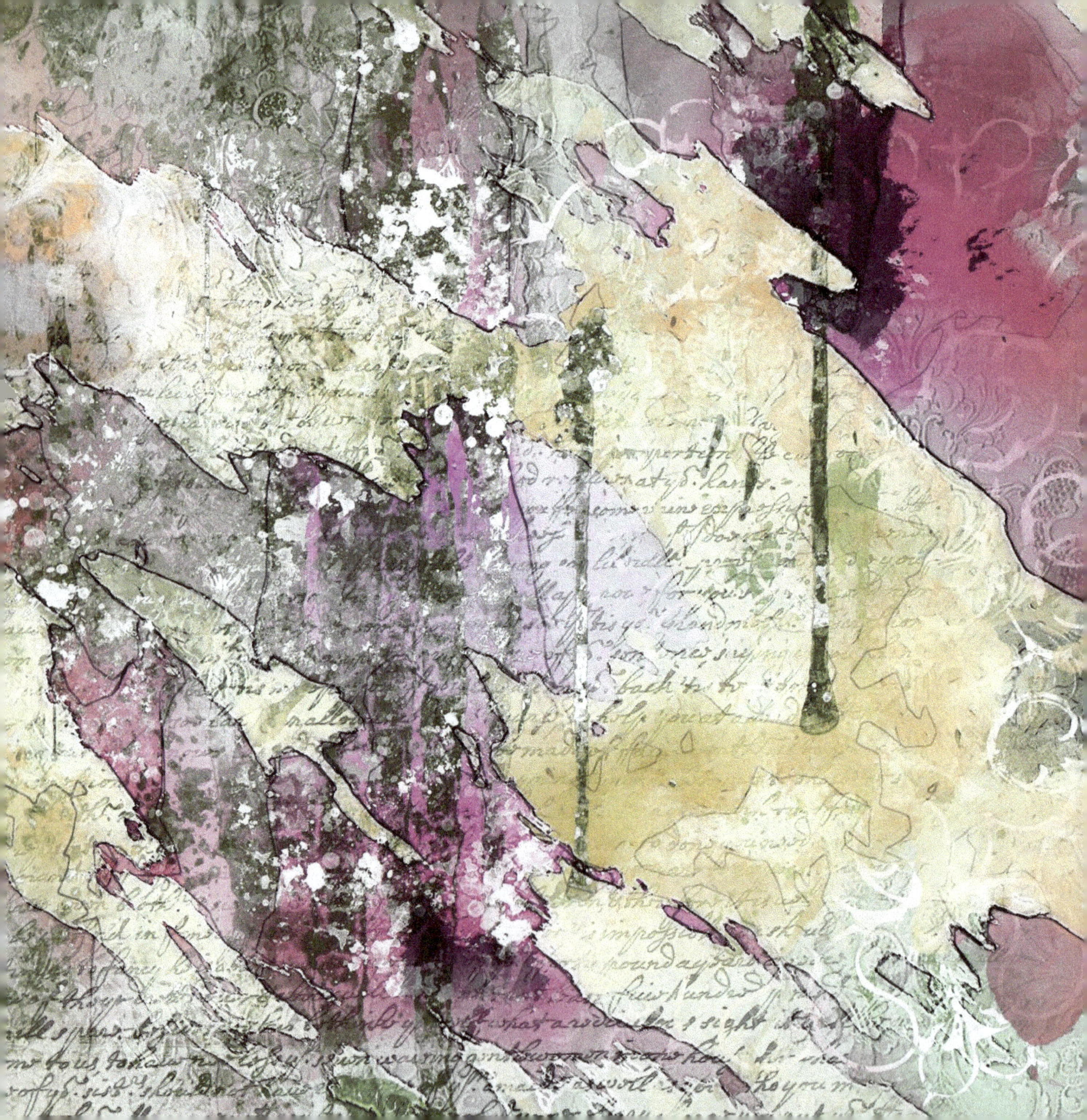

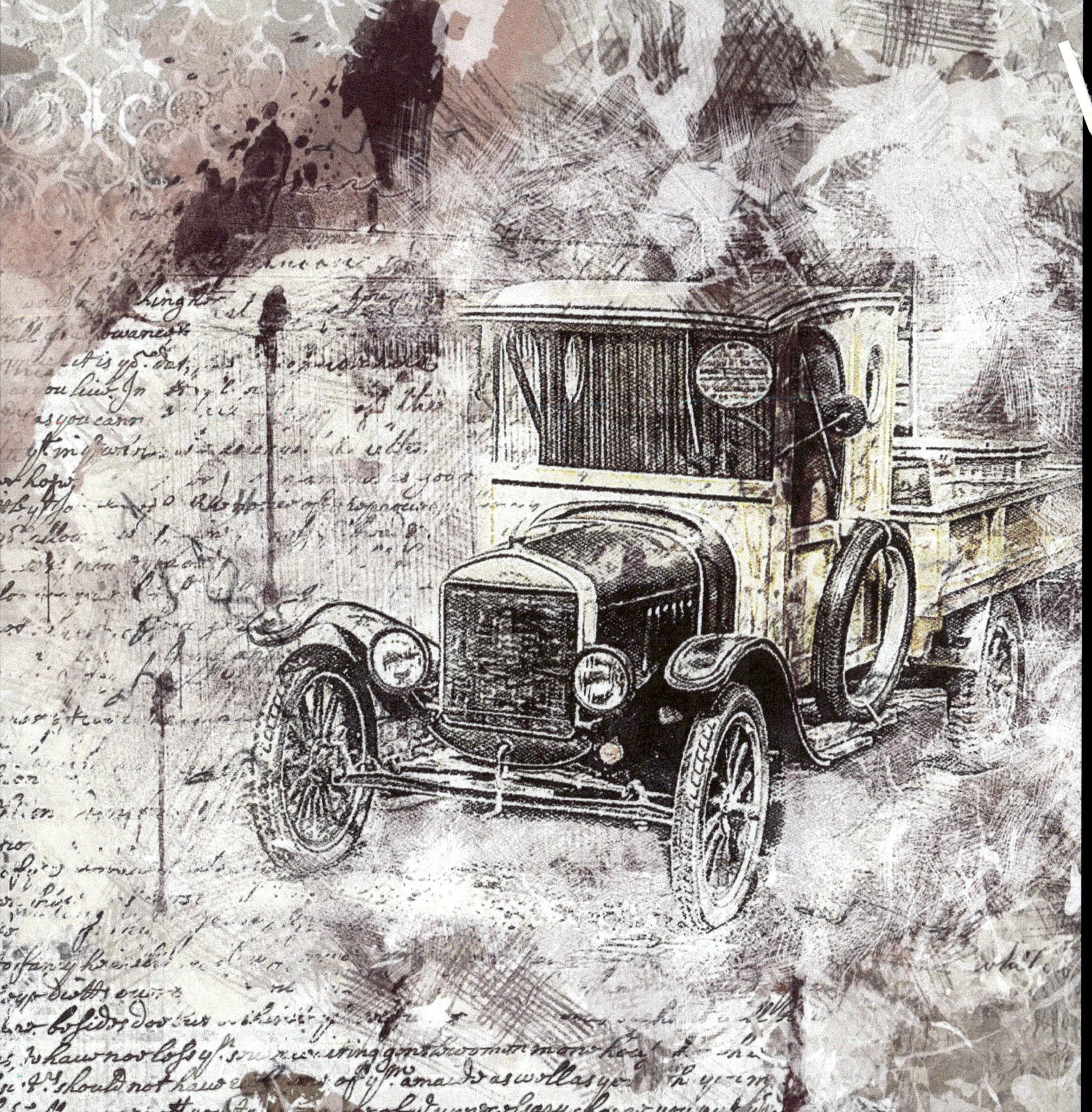

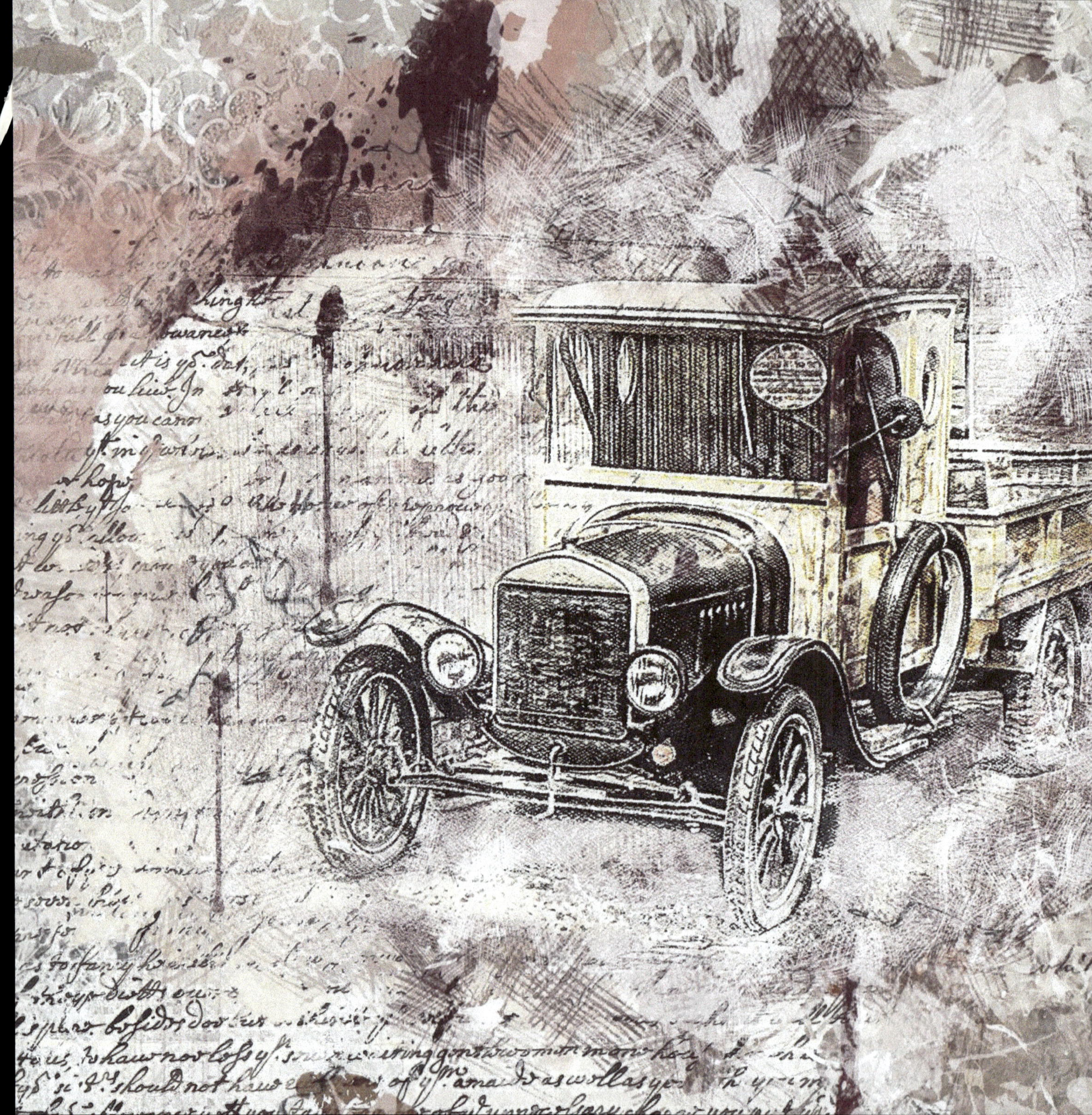

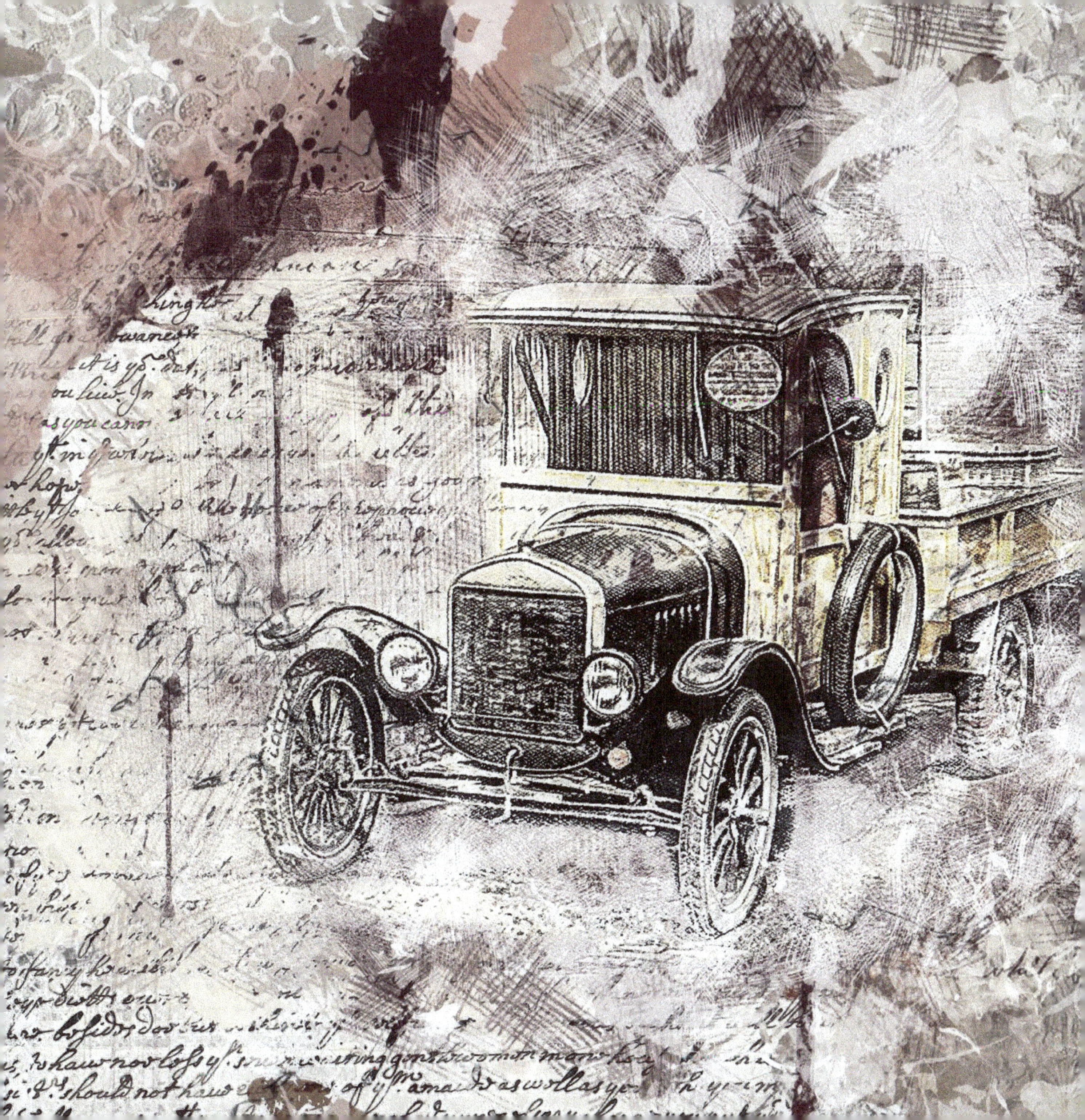

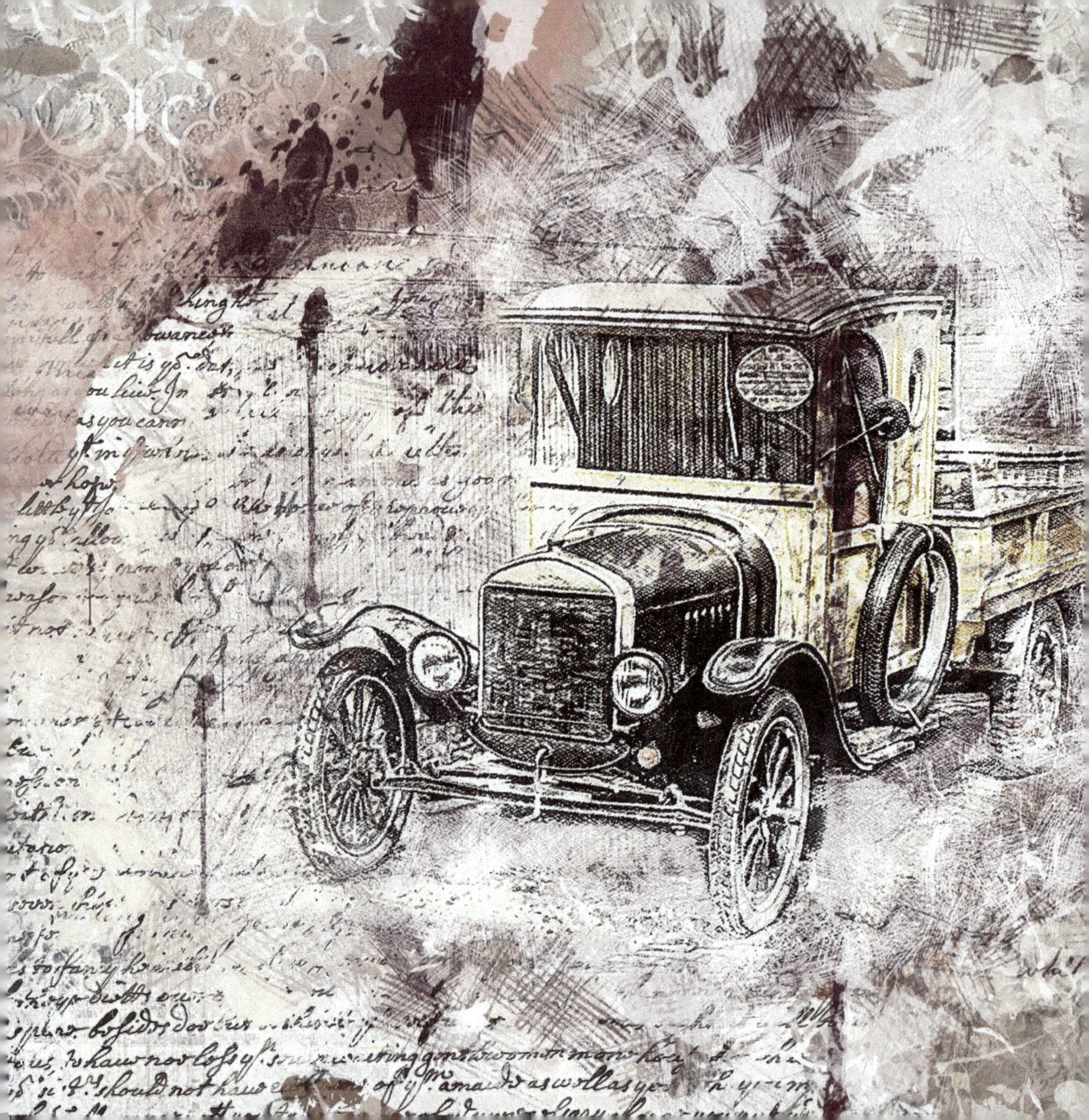

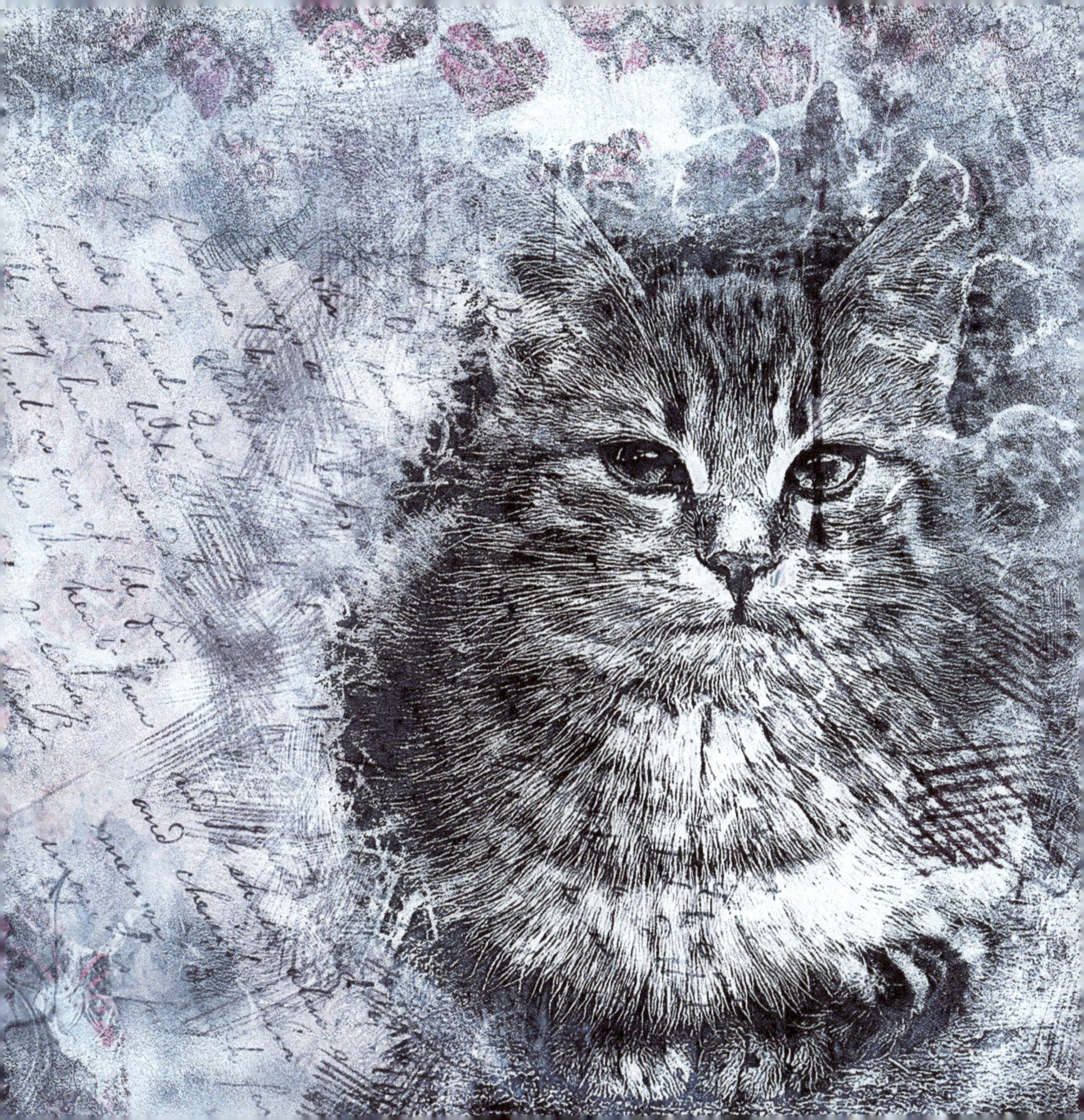

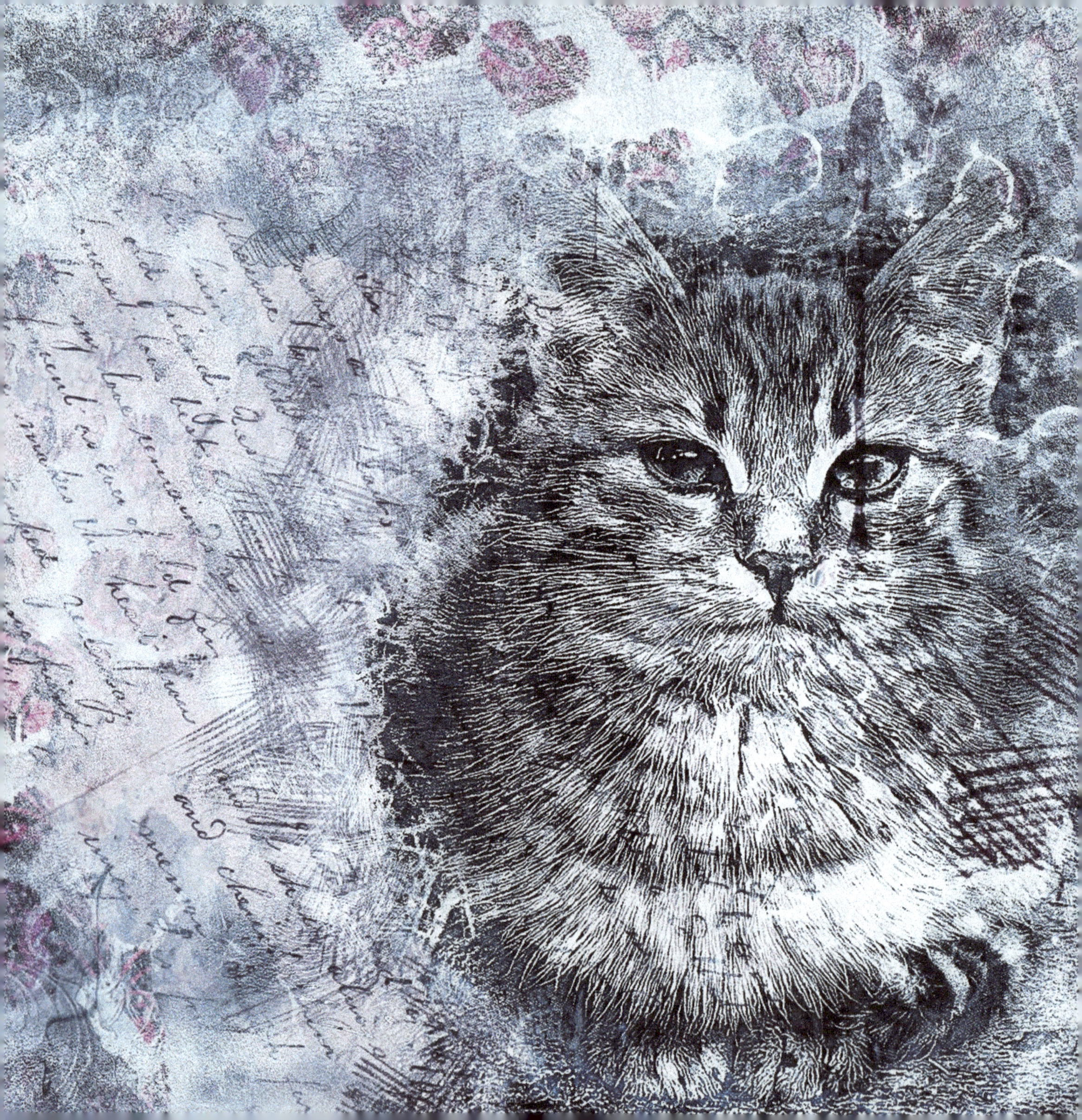

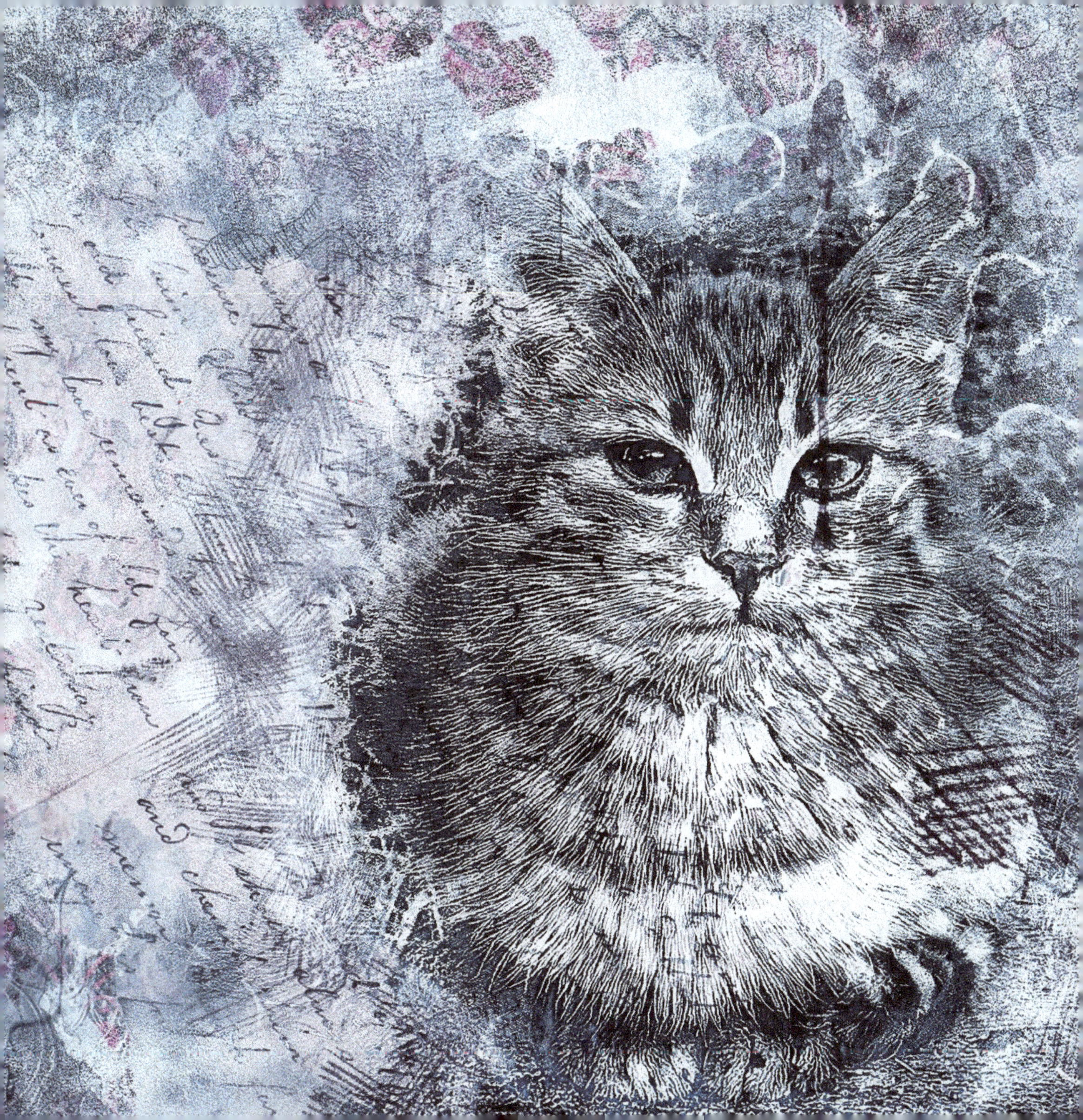

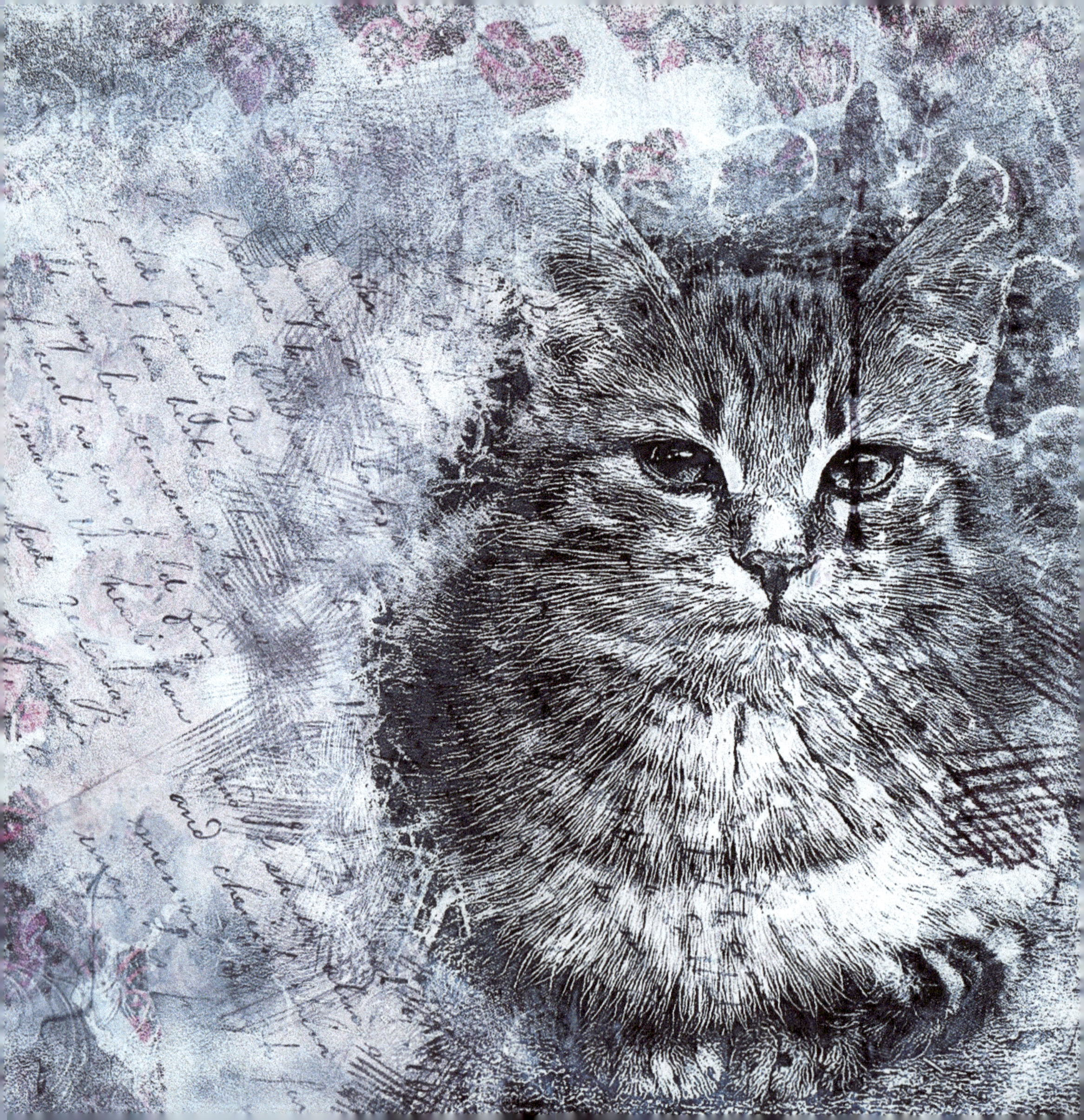

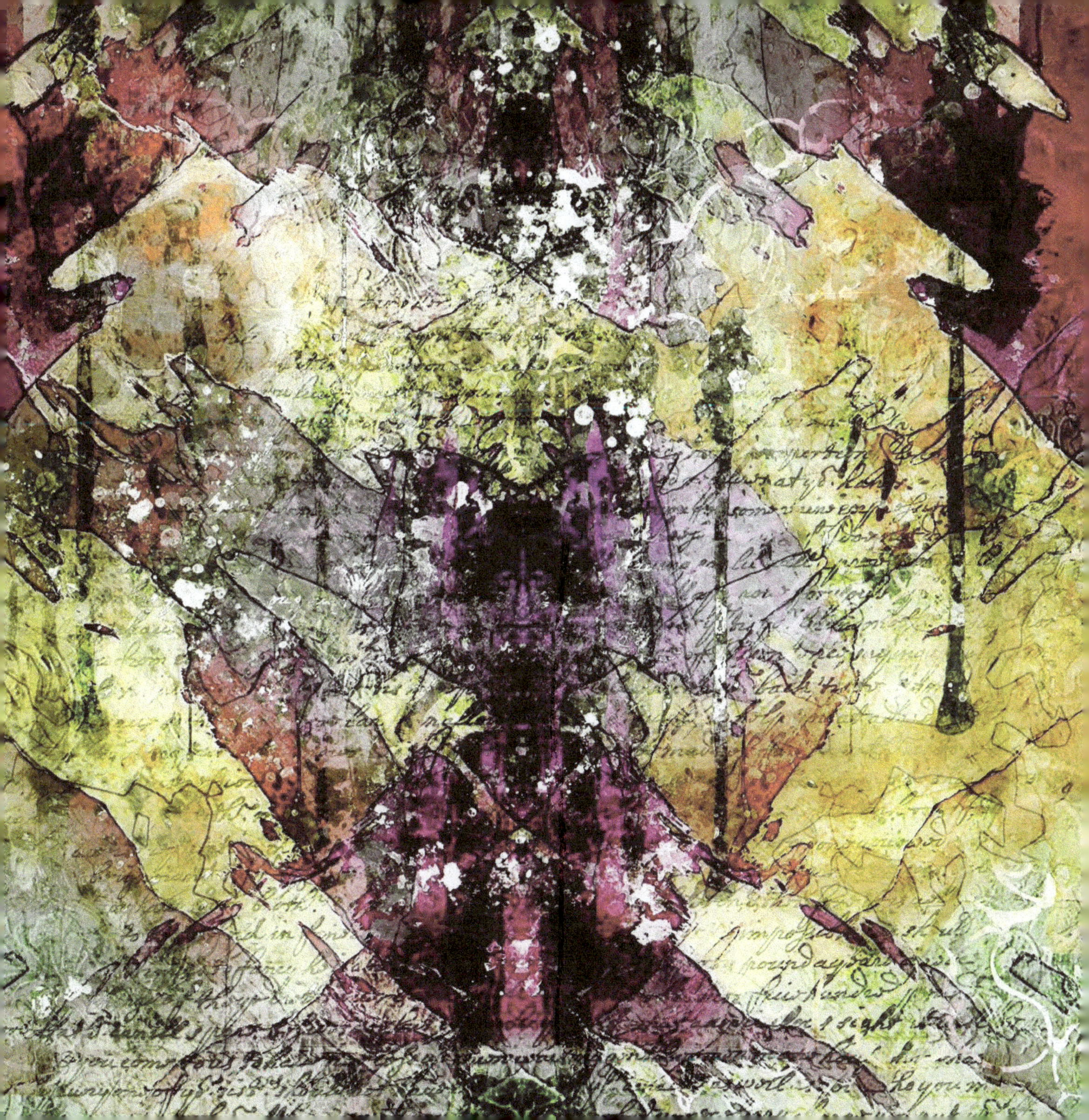

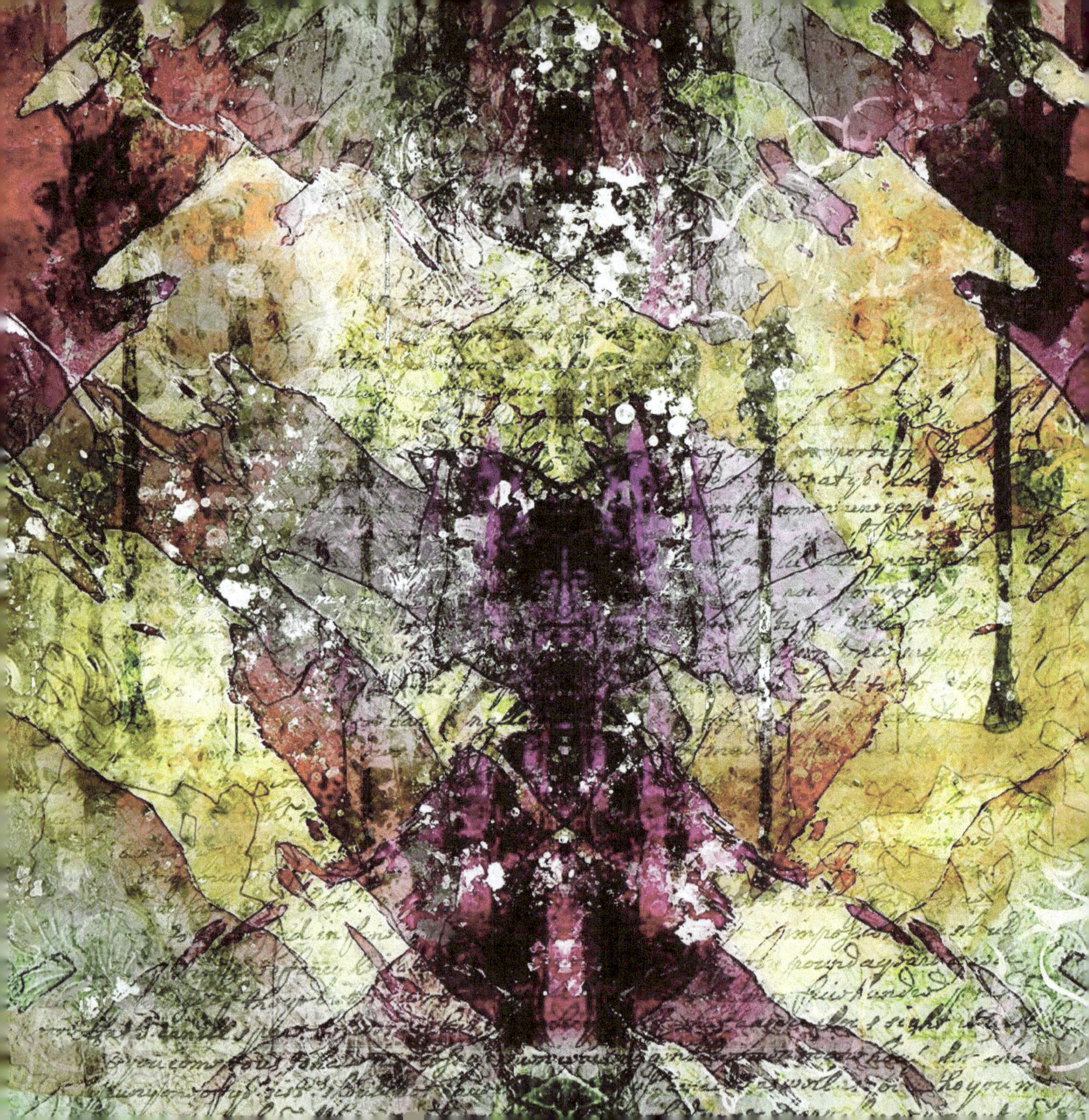

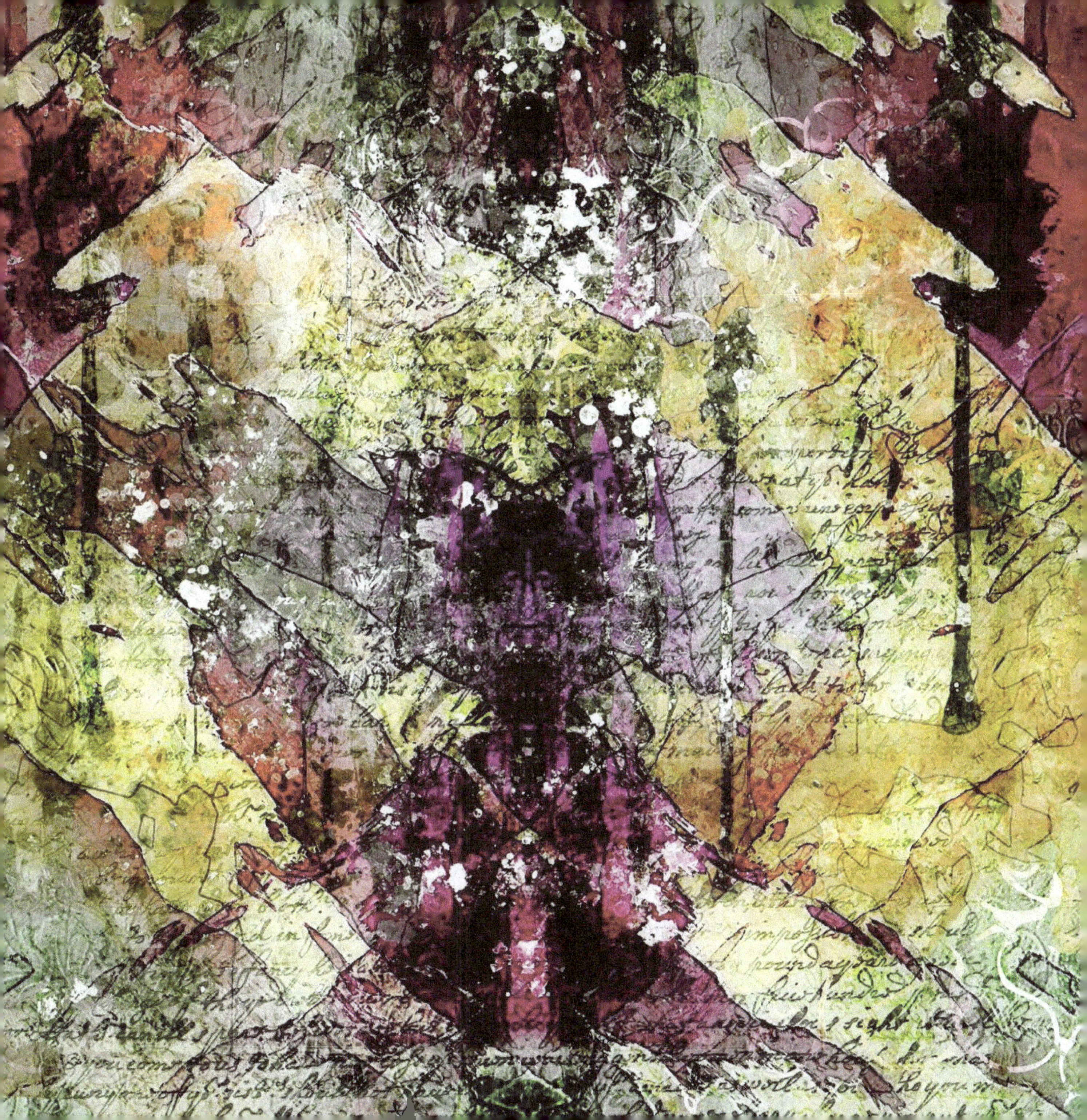

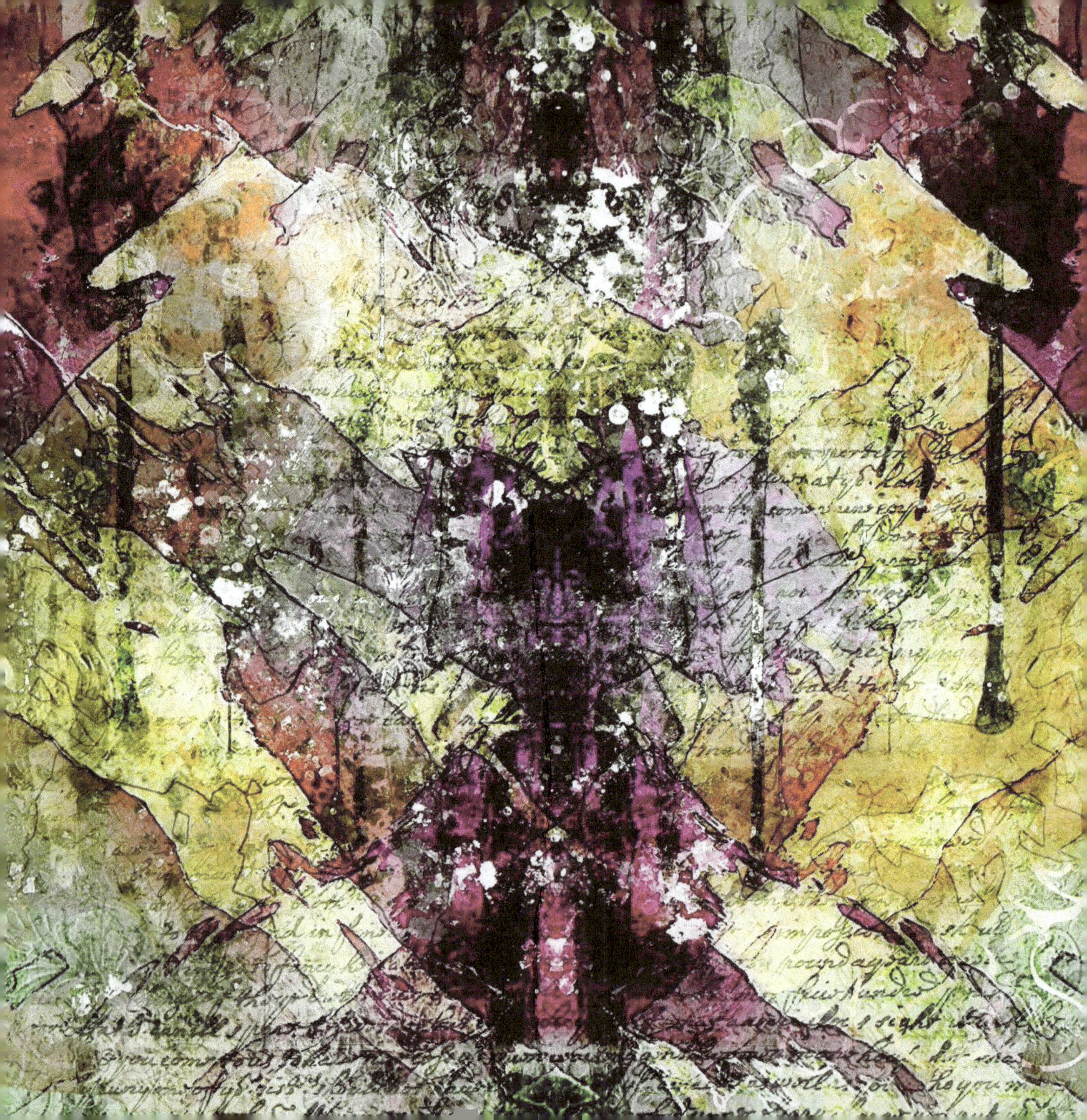

are prohibee par nos loix [illegible]
[illegible] Delisle [illegible]
[illegible]

[illegible] [illegible]
[illegible] hing her self to make [illegible] you in
[illegible] wance & you toivor als her [illegible]
it is yo[r] duty on all occasions to p[illegible]
one here I must tell you tis to her [illegible]
as you cannot but [illegible]
[illegible] whole bred [illegible]
[illegible] make her such [illegible]
[illegible] to be in [illegible]
[illegible] aim to be [illegible]
[illegible] solution [illegible]
[illegible] moist it is [illegible]
[illegible] int appear [illegible] my [illegible]
[illegible] tis m[y] opinion if yo[u] [illegible]
[illegible] law [illegible] allowance in yo[ur] [illegible]
[illegible] es end you [illegible] if care [illegible]
[illegible] all commendations for a you [illegible]
[illegible] if ever yo[u] bestowd [illegible]
[illegible] I thank [illegible]
[illegible] was [illegible] if [illegible] what you
[illegible] [illegible] you are a [illegible]
[illegible] in g[illegible] [illegible] for example [illegible]
[illegible] he is her to allow [illegible] way [illegible] a you [illegible]
[illegible] [illegible] [illegible] hunder [illegible]
[illegible] doo [illegible] [illegible] sight [illegible]
[illegible] you s[illegible] [illegible] good [illegible] more [illegible]
[illegible] these [illegible] [illegible] as will as you [illegible]

[illegible] prohibée par nos loix [illegible]

[illegible]

[illegible] king himself to make you [illegible]
[illegible] you to one also for that [illegible]
it is your duty on all occasions to pay [illegible]
[illegible] you [illegible]
[illegible] as you cannot but [illegible]
[illegible]
[illegible] my resolution [illegible]
[illegible]
[illegible] it apparent in [illegible]
[illegible] opinion of you [illegible]
[illegible] an [illegible] allowance in your [illegible]
[illegible] and you very [illegible]
[illegible] small commendation for a [illegible]
[illegible] if ever you best [illegible] for [illegible]
[illegible] I thank'd [illegible]
[illegible]
[illegible] for the [illegible]
[illegible]
[illegible]

lice prohibee par nos [illegible]
and [illegible] Delisle to the [illegible]
[illegible]

[illegible]
[illegible]
[illegible]hing herself to make you in [illegible]
[illegible] you to [illegible] as her [illegible]
it is y[illegible] duty on all occasions to [illegible]
one [illegible] I must tell you tis do her [illegible]
as you cannot but [illegible]
in y[illegible] whole conduct [illegible]
[illegible] make her such [illegible]
[illegible]
[illegible] you ailm to bring [illegible]
[illegible]
[illegible] my resolution [illegible]
[illegible]
[illegible] plainly apparent in y[illegible]
[illegible] tis my opinion if you [illegible]
[illegible] allowance in y[illegible]
[illegible] end y[illegible] you y[illegible] can [illegible]
[illegible] commendations for a you[illegible]
[illegible] if ever y[illegible] bestowd [illegible]
[illegible] I thank [illegible] for [illegible]
[illegible]
[illegible] you are admit [illegible]
[illegible] for tis impos[illegible]
[illegible] no [illegible]
[illegible]
[illegible] doo [illegible]
[illegible]
[illegible] was well as you [illegible]

[illegible] prohibee par nos loix [illegible]
[illegible] Janvier Delisle [illegible]
[illegible]

[illegible] hing her self to make you [illegible]
[illegible] you to wine also her [illegible]
it is yo.r duty on all occasions to [illegible]
[illegible] I must tell you tis to her [illegible]
as you cannot but be [illegible]
[illegible] whole friend [illegible]
[illegible] make her such [illegible]
[illegible] be no [illegible]
[illegible] you aim to bring [illegible]
[illegible]
[illegible] solution
[illegible]
[illegible] pl into appearance in y.e [illegible]
[illegible] tis no opinion if you [illegible]
[illegible] lane malbowne in yo.r [illegible]
[illegible] end y.e vs. y.t can [illegible]
[illegible] small commendations for a your [illegible]
[illegible] ever y.t bestowd on [illegible]
[illegible] the I thank [illegible]
[illegible]
[illegible]

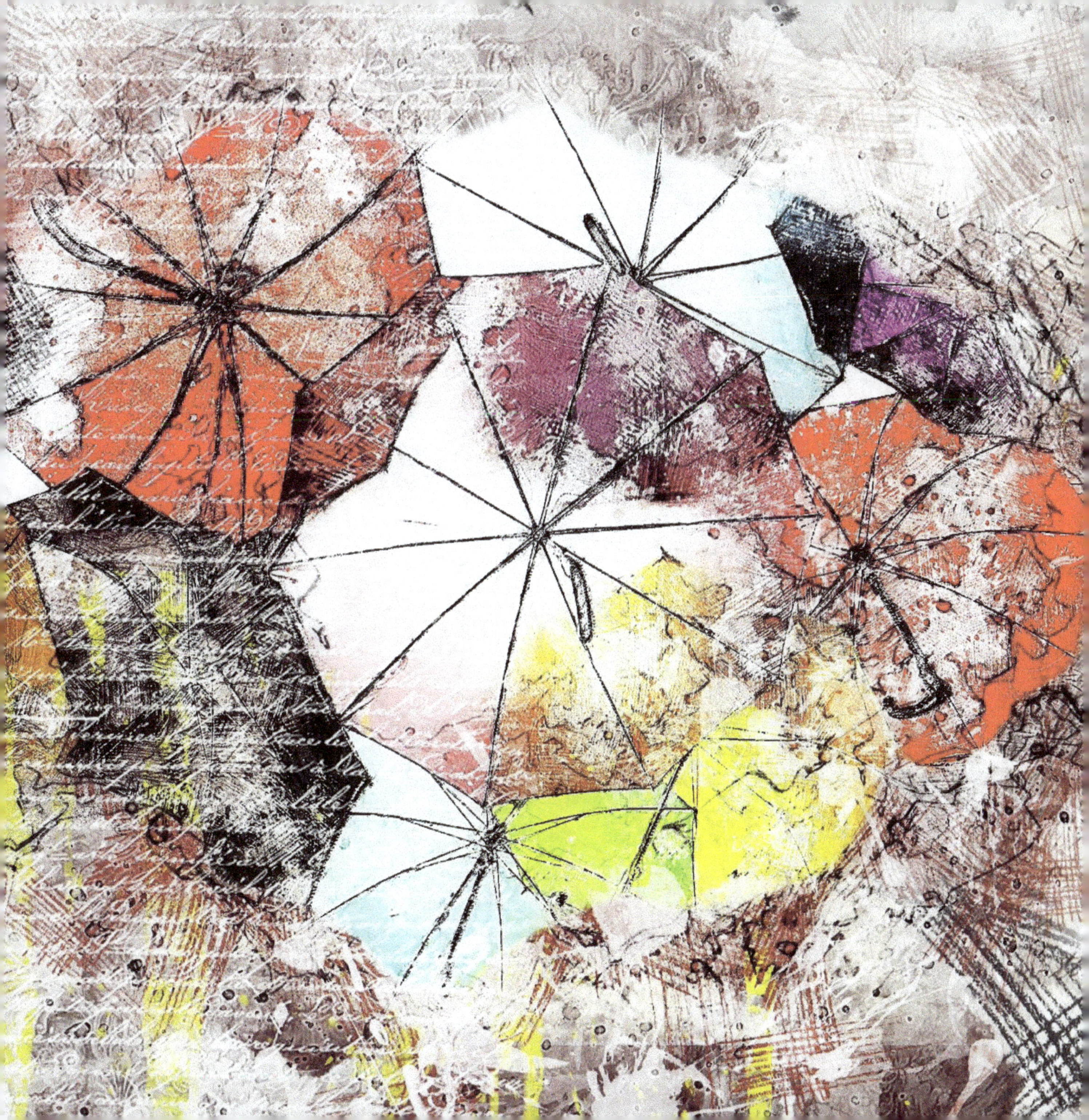

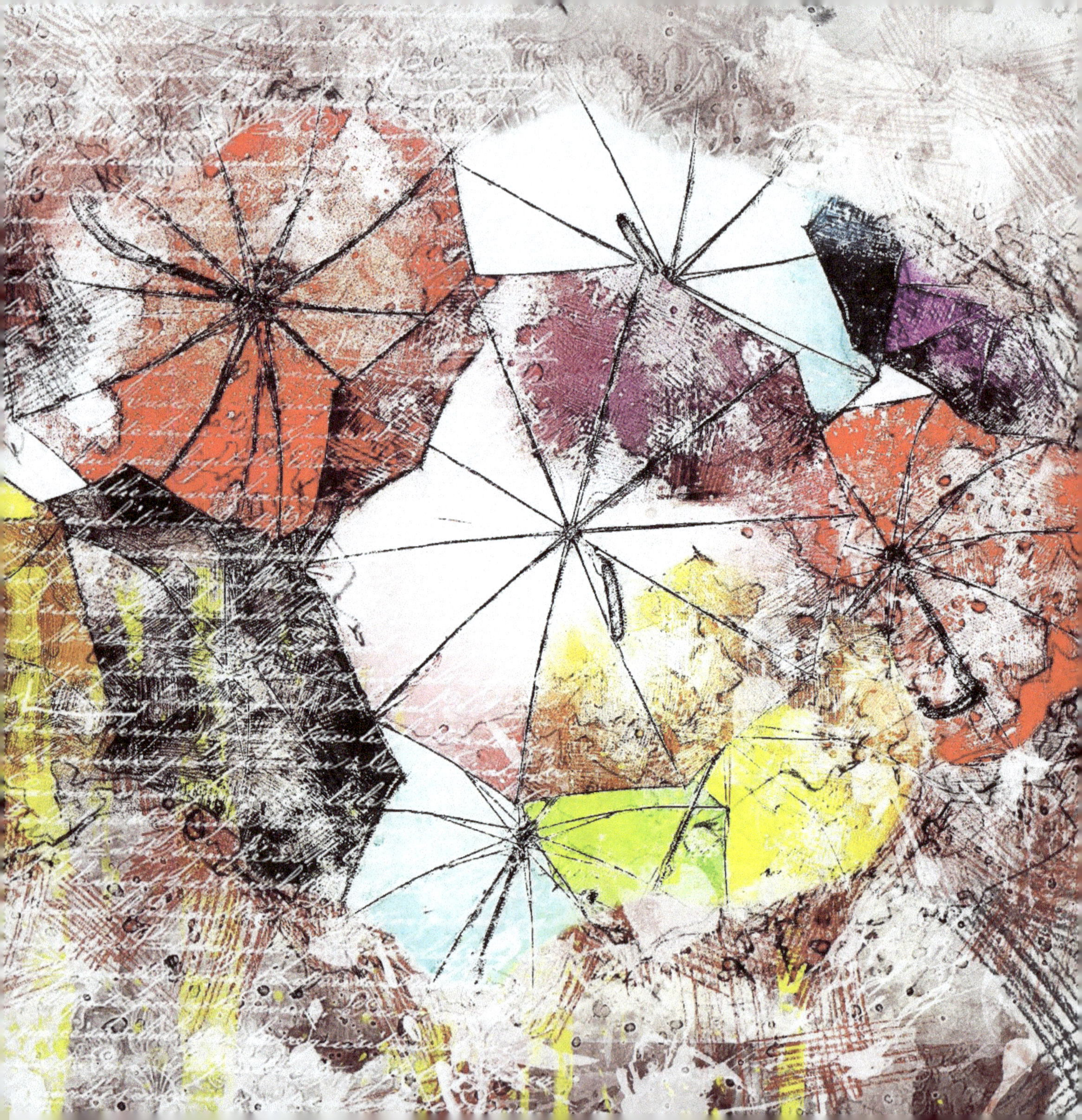

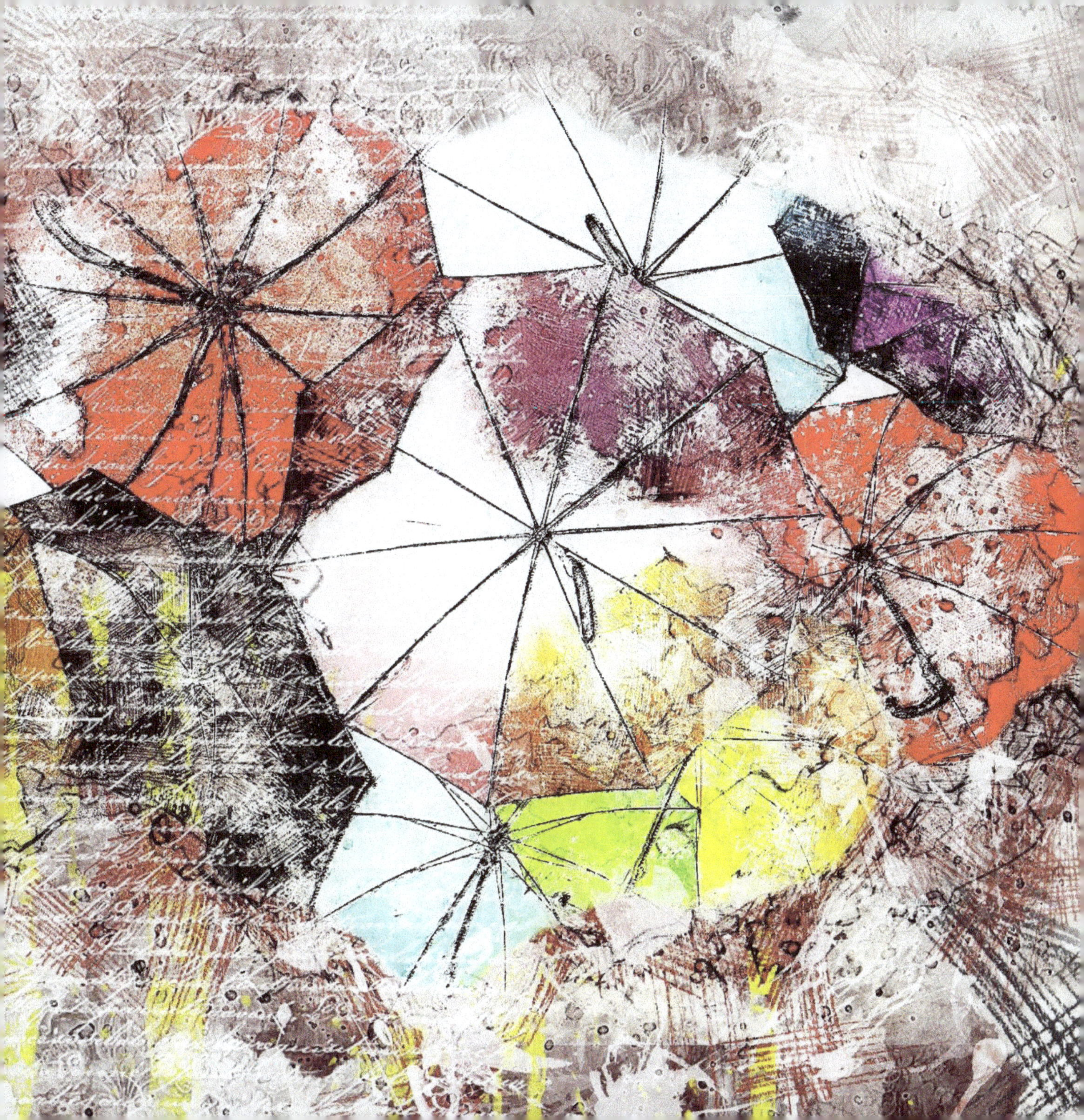

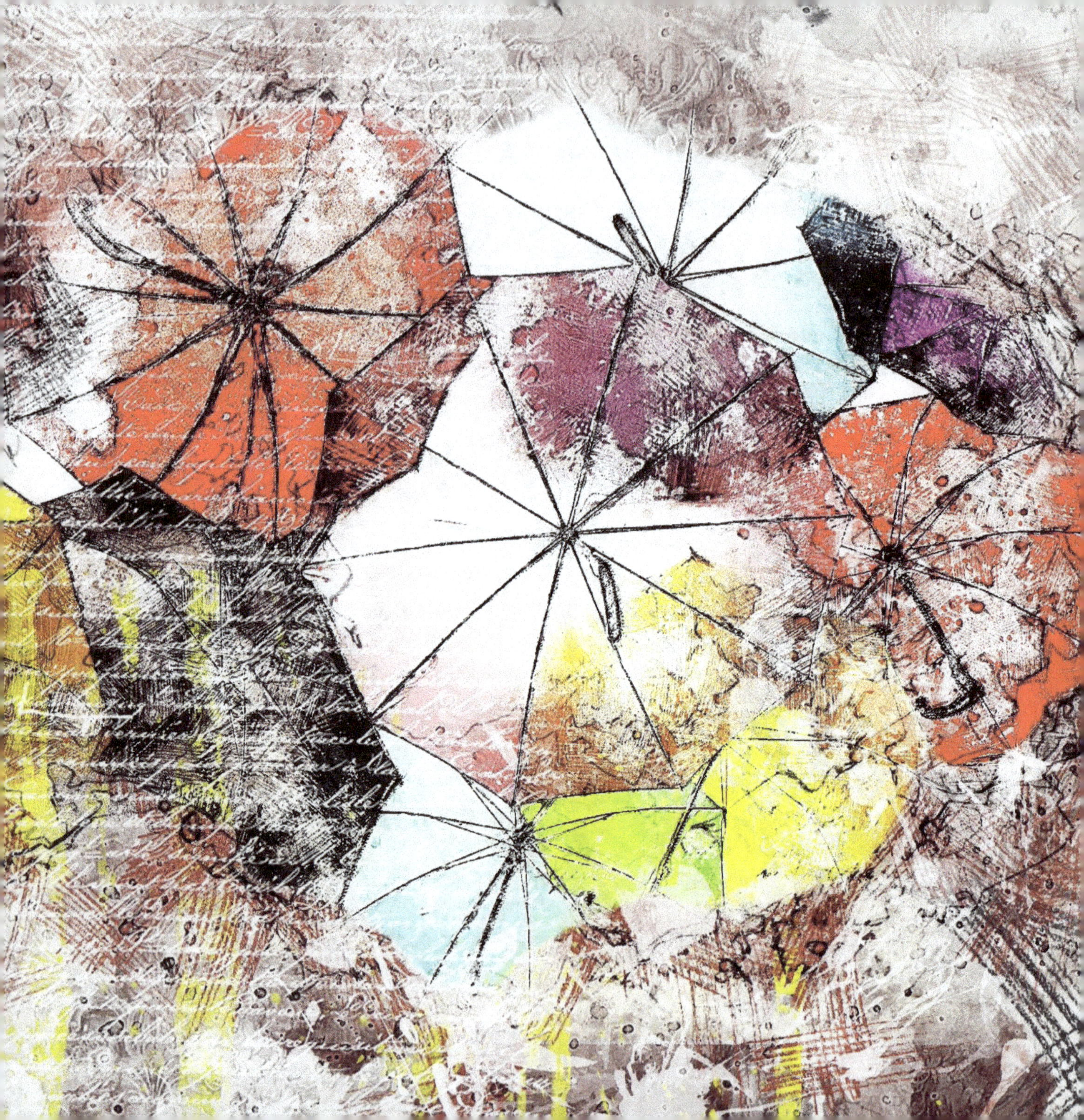